THE RESOURCES OF MUSIC

Vocal Score and Commentary

Wilfrid Mellers

Professor of Music, University of York

CAMBRIDGE
AT THE UNIVERSITY PRESS
1969

CAMBRIDGE UNIVERSITY PRESS
Cambridge, New York, Melbourne, Madrid, Cape Town,
Singapore, São Paulo, Delhi, Tokyo, Mexico City

Cambridge University Press
The Edinburgh Building, Cambridge CB2 8RU, UK

Published in the United States of America by Cambridge University Press, New York

www.cambridge.org
Information on this title: www.cambridge.org/9780521072632

First published 1969
Re-issued 2011

A catalogue record for this publication is available from the British Library

ISBN 978-0-521-07263-2 Paperback

CONTENTS

ACKNOWLEDGEMENTS

Thanks are due to Sir Maurice Bowra, George Weidenfeld and Nicolson Ltd. and The World Publishing Co. Inc. for permission to use poems from *Primitive Song* by Sir Maurice Bowra.

INTRODUCTION

A School Project by way of an Experiment in Composition

This work, called *Life Cycle*, may be considered as an artistic creation in terms of music and theatre; or as a project for schools, involving the interrelationship of departments (music, English, visual arts, crafts, physics, perhaps geography and history in their sociological aspects). Its success as a school project will depend on the willingness of departments to cooperate with one another; and to some extent, of course, on the size of the school and the time available.

The poems which initiated the work are by the Gaban pygmies and the eskimos; they trace the cycle of human experience from pre-birth to death. For the pygmies and eskimos—and for any 'primitive' people—words are inseparable from action (of work, play or religious ritual); and action is inseparable from music. It follows that although, as a composer, I wrote this piece basically as a musical work it is also, in the widest and deepest sense, theatre; and its ideal realization will include, along with the music, dance, mime and drama. These visual arts in turn involve decor, costume, and masks.[1] In the Commentary I have indicated possible collaborations between music teacher and specialists in English, drama, and the visual arts. Both staff and pupils will be able to think of many more.

The degree of theatrical commitment may, of course, vary according to the resources available; and if need be the work may be performed merely as concert music, so long as the performers approach it 'theatrically'. A few preliminary remarks should be made about the piece's musical substance. The first is that I wrote the music simply as a setting of the texts. While I naturally knew that the poems traced the cycle of human experience, I didn't consciously attempt to use different and developing musical 'materials' for each piece: so that what I have said in the Commentary is a rationalization after the event. Something like this, the Commentary says, seems to happen in a composer's subconscious mind; and evolution of musical resources occurs in this work not by deliberate intention or choice, but because the verses are concerned with evolution. Even fairly sophisticated procedures like the quotation of earlier movements at the end of 'Ageing-Song' occurred spontaneously: though after I had noticed it was happening, I made conscious use of it, as any composer would.

Added to this is a related point. You are involved in the work as musical participants, and sometimes I suggest that you contribute not merely as performers, but also as composers or makers. When this happens you should regard my suggestions as no more than that; you are at liberty to alter them, or to make counter-suggestions which can be discussed among you, and with your teacher-conductor.

There are also many different ways of performing the written parts. In so far as the piece can be thought of as working material for school use, as well as a 'finished' artistic creation, you may regard it as a basis for experiment. What is offered in printed form is not the full orchestral score, but a short or 'vocal' score indicating the original instrumentation, yet capable of being rescored for such resources as you have available. While you should aim at producing something comparable with the original tone-colours, it is more important to create something that sounds effective, given the resources you are writing for. The labour of copying out the parts will be an essential part of the project: there is no better way of getting to know how music works! Since most of the pieces are scored for relatively small groups of instruments (i.e. brass, wind or strings), the task of adaptation should not be too difficult. I offer some hints in the Notes on Performance; and should perhaps add that if you cannot produce the forces necessary to perform all the movements, this does not invalidate the project.

The definitive version is for speaker (with microphone), a large mixed chorus, a small semi-chorus of trebles and altos, a noise or 'effects' chorus, a baritone soloist, a normal full orchestra with large percussion section, an orchestra of bells, and electronic tapes. Score and parts of this version are available on hire, and I hope it may be used whenever some gala occasion prompts a performance—

preferably, though not essentially, with some dance projection. Very large schools could probably produce the necessary forces, or two or more schools might combine—especially since the work calls for the cooperation of girls and boys. The orchestration, even of the full version, may be modified where necessary: for instance, the score employs the customary four horns, but you could make do with two horns plus two bassoons or clarinets.

The instrumental parts, and to some degree the vocal parts, are not all easy and in the nature of the project they get more difficult as the work proceeds. Good players are required for some of the later pieces, and if you have not got them there is no reason why you should not bring in outsiders—teachers, friends and so on.

How long you take over *Life Cycle* as a school project depends on many variable factors. If there is a good deal of collaboration between school departments there will be many subsidiary projects fanning out from the central one. The poems, for instance, could lead to an investigation of the nature of primitive song and its relationship to other poetry; mask-making and dancing could involve studies in anthropology and religion as well as drama. I suggest reading material, and lines of enquiry in the Commentary. In its theatrical aspects this project may be correlated with approaches suggested by Peter Slade's *Child Drama*, John Hodgson's *Improvisation in Drama*, and V. Bruce's *Lord of the Dance*. In its musical aspects the project is intended as a complement to *Sound and Silence* by Peter Aston and John Paynter. If you have already used this book you will be familiar with the approach to music as theatre, and will be able to proceed pretty rapidly with the creation of music out of nature-noises, bird and animal cries, etc. If you have not used the book there will be more for the teacher to adapt and invent, and you will take proportionally longer over the various stages. The essence of the project lies, however, in its flexibility; I hope that as education it will lead you on voyages of discovery at whatever level, and that as creation it will offer you an experience of involvement, whether you are singing or playing the difficult bits, dancing or miming, or merely clapping or yelling. Certainly it has been fun to write.

University of York
November 1967

W.M.

LIFE CYCLE

A cantata for young people

For two choirs and orchestra; or for ad hoc instrumentation

Vocal Score

The words are from the pygmies and eskimos, translated by
Sir Maurice Bowra in his book, *Primitive Song*

The 'definitive' version of this work is scored for

A speaker, preferably using microphone (movements 1 and 9).

A singing chorus, as large as possible, in unison or two parts except for a brief (optional) four-part section at the end. 'Broken' voices (tenors and basses) should be included as well as trebles and altos, so that the music will of course sound in doubled octaves. Preferably boys should outnumber girls in this chorus (movements 1, 2, 3, 7 and 9).

A (more expert) semi-chorus of girls' voices, with a few boy trebles added if desired. This semi-chorus is responsible for most of the musical 'substance'. A few short passages may be sung by soloists from the semi-chorus (movements 2, 3, 4, 6, 7, 8, 9).

A noise or 'effects' chorus which is not required to sing pitched intervals. This chorus should be roughly half the size of the large singing chorus.

A high baritone (or low tenor) soloist. He can be an imported professional, but a teenage student would be better. His two solos are not easy, but a highly polished performance is not necessary nor even, perhaps, desirable (movements 5 and 8).

A normal full orchestra; which can be modified, in ways indicated in the preface to the Commentary, according to the resources available. When the full orchestral version is used, the players should not be grouped in the traditional manner but in separate choirs of brass, woodwind and strings, which sometimes combine but more often function independently. The percussion section must be large: though alternative instruments may be substituted for those indicated in the score.

Extra percussion players on stage, to work with:

Masked dancers and mimers, the number of which will vary according to the space and resources available. If choreographed, the work will of course require a producer.

Microphones, contact microphones and electronic tapes, to be employed as indicated in the score.

A 'campanology' orchestra, placed separately from the main orchestra. A wide variety of bell-sonorities is required; experiment with alternative methods of producing the appropriate effects. Orchestral chimes are needed for some movements but will not do for all. A set of hand bells suspended would be useful, reinforced by Orff glockenspiels, xylophones, metallophones, finger cymbals and triangles. Electronic assistance would be effective in places. The campanology enunciates the mode, scale, figure on which each piece is based.

I

Nature-Song

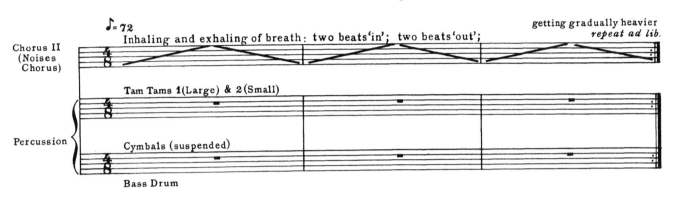

* The declamation of speaker and of Chorus II need not be strictly in the time-values indicated (which follow verbal rhythm), but the first beat of each bar should synchronize with the conductor, who in this movement acts as a metronome merely.

C.U.P.

* At this point chorus turns its 'sshes' into snake, insect and bird noises, *senza tempo.*

Leading to:

6

FREE SECTION: duration to be decided by conductor   (no beat)

* The creature-calls on wind instruments should enter separately and continue independently, long enough to build up a furious hubbub.
  The vocal improvisations should be stimulated to greater frenzy by the instruments.

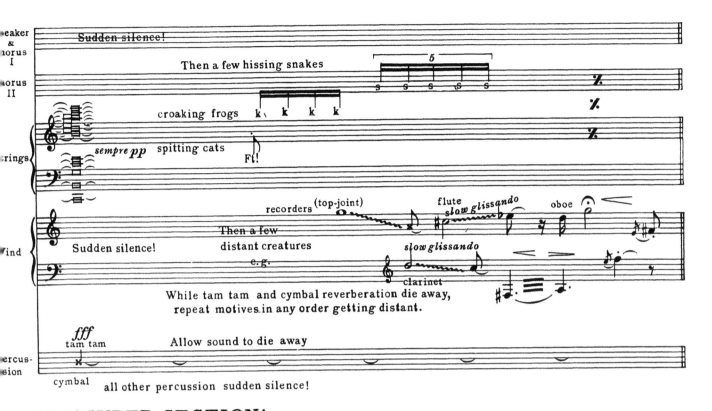

MEASURED SECTION!

conductor resumes pulse-beat ♪=72

8

CARILLON 1

Segue No.2

Sun-Song

The bar-lines are for the conductor's convenience only: the piece should feel unmeasured.

C.U.P.

CARILLON 2

3
Birth-Song

Temple blocks

CARILLON 3

END

Bells and chimes (not synchronized), slower and slower

improvise on these notes

Segue No.4

4
Sleep-Song

20

C.U.P.

CARILLON 4

C.U.P.

Segue No 5

5
Love-Song

CARILLON 5

6
Bride-Song

CARILLON 6

Improvise on these figures not synchronized

End with triangle roll leading into no. 7

7
Living-Song

Segue No 8

8

Ageing-Song

9
Death-Song

38

C.U.P.

C.U.P.

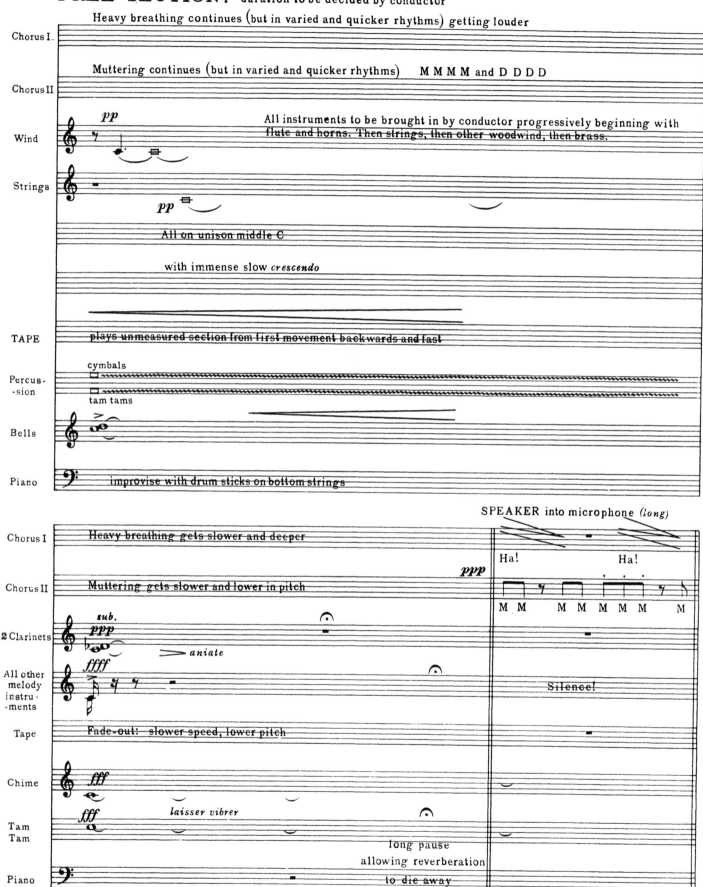

NOTES ON PERFORMANCE

1 Nature-Song

Since the performing techniques are here unconventional, the printed score gives fairly detailed instructions. The Harmonic Series chord, sustained more or less throughout the piece, calls for a large number of strings. If you have not got them, use the alternative 'skeleton' chord, on strings or organ. If necessary this chord could be played on piano, with pedals, very softly reiterated; but it really needs continuously sustained tone. The long-held wind chords may be played on any instruments you have, or even on piano, with pedal. Use as many of the wind-instrument bird and animal cries as you can; or invent others.

2 Sun-Song

This song calls for as large a number of voices as possible; the occasional *divisi* in the vocal part provide alternatives to the high notes for those who find them uncomfortable. Sing with 'open' tone, wild, not too beautiful, and use as many instrumental doublings and drones as you like. These instrumental parts really ought to be brass, as in the full score; but flutes, oboes, clarinets—*not* strings—could be substituted for them. Once again, if necessary, piano (playing in octaves) could double the vocal line.

The pitched bells should preferably be hand-bells suspended, reinforced by glockenspiel. Chimes would be less suitable. The triangle must be large and brilliant. Other small hand drums may be substituted for bongos.

3 Birth-Song

The vocal tone should be really savage, raucous and throaty, the singing not so far off from the shouting: the pygmies make a no less legitimate sound than English cathedral trebles! Use as many voices as possible for both choruses, with as much instrumental doubling as you like. Piano, played percussively, could be substituted for some of the brass (it does remarkably well as trombones). Do not use strings except in the places indicated. Any hard hand drum can be substituted for bongos.

4 Sleep-Song

This must be sung by the girls' semi-chorus; others may add a humming *obligato* if desired. More conventionally expressive singing is required here; even the 'beautiful voice' would not come amiss. The original scoring should present few problems. The guitar is not essential, but you may well have one around. It would be quite effective—in the absence of strings—to play the *ostinato* on piano, both pedals down, and guitar, perhaps with a single drone C on cello. The instrumental coda, however, really needs expressive string playing. The bassoon could be a cello.

5 Love-Song

This must be sung by tenor or baritone solo, possibly doubled by oboes. No part for chorus here, for the song, though celebrative, is intimate: addressed by one boy to a particular girl. The vocal style should be free and wild, but

more beautifully expressive than the 'Sun-Song'; and the last stanza should be more 'artistically' sung than the first.

Horns are desirable for the drone, and if there are only two they will have to stagger their breathing. Strings may be used for the drone, but only as a makeshift. The melodic arabesques in the instrumental parts must be on trumpet and/or woodwind. They are quite difficult, and may be simplified if need be. The pitched bells should preferably be suspended handbells, doubled by glockenspiel. Chimes are not desirable.

6 Bride-Song

The lament-aria should be sung by the semi-chorus of picked voices. The others may vocalize (ah, oh, etc.) with the instrumental *ostinato* figure if they wish. The vocal style should be simple, yet very expressive: rather folk-like, though it could not be a folk song because it is too 'harmonic'.

The original scoring, or something like it, should present few problems, except for the sustained string chord in the middle section. It is essential to play all the notes of this chord: so divide it between strings, woodwind and horns if necessary.

7 Living-Song

The vocal style is now quite sophisticated, jazzy: so the piece is best sung by the semi-chorus of picked voices, with everyone joining in the 'Avayas' and the clapping. Keep the percussion pattern absolutely regular! The piece is rhythmically quite tricky, and you should feel that it is difficult, yet happy-making, to get it right. A good pianist can make an effect with the woodwind parts, reinforced by *pizzicato* strings and/or guitar; but this would not work so well in the instrumental coda.

8 Ageing-Song

This is, and is meant to be, the most difficult piece, which must be sung by a tenor or baritone soloist. No chorus here, because part of the point is the loneliness of age, the decay of connectedness with the tribe. The soloist ought to be something of an actor too. The instrumental parts can hardly dispense with two violins and two clarinets, with horns and/or strings to play the drone-chord and its extensions. But again a good pianist could help out, if need be.

9 Death-Song

The vocal style, to begin with, should be remote, other-worldly, without *vibrato*. It should become more normal at the stanza introducing Man, and may be conventionally 'beautiful' for the four-part invocation of the god Khvum. Strings are essential for the note-clusters, the only alternative being very soft stops on organ. But you might be able to invent some vocal substitute, using microtones fanning out from a single tone; and voices might also substitute for the long-held notes on wind instruments. Experiment with the tape effects at the end. The heavy breathing, slowed down, could be awe-inspiring indeed!

THE RESOURCES OF MUSIC

COMMENTARY

What is music? What are its materials? What is it for?

We are going to explore these questions—though we shall not arrive at any final answers to them—by way of practical experiment. I am a composer, and you could be too, because creating in sound is a natural human activity: so I shall make a musical composition and shall try to describe how it evolves, within the mind, and from the world we live in; and I shall give you an opportunity to take part in it both as performers and as 'makers'—to use the old-fashioned but accurate phrase. Since we want to begin at the beginning, we shall imagine that we are aboriginal peoples who, living remote from our complex industrial civilization, have much in common with all of us in childhood. Indeed their experience, or most of it, has been ours; so we shall learn something about ourselves, as well as about music, in taking some runes, incantations, play-songs and work-songs from the Gaban pygmies and the eskimos (one hot people and one cold), and in considering what the musical implications of the verses might be.[2]

We shall start with a song about the natural world —the universe of winds and waters, rocks and plants, birds and beasts—as it is 'in itself.' Of course we cannot really do this, since we can experience the world only through our consciousness. None the less primitive peoples, and we as children, have a sense of mystery and awe in contemplating the otherness of the natural world, and this comes through in this incantation. We shall read the poem out loud:

> The tree has given its fruit, and the fruit is good to eat.
> Oh! Oh! Oh! Yele, yao, yao!
> The day is bright and the night is black.
> Say nothing, do not speak, those who pass this way!
> Oh! Oh! Oh! yele, yao, yao!
> The fruit turns to dust at the foot of the tree,
> The animal runs and man eats it,
> The bird flies and man eats it,
> The fish darts and man eats it.
> Oh! Oh! Oh! yele, yao, yao!
> Say nothing, do not speak, those who pass this way.
> Oh! Oh! Oh! yele, yao, yao!

This has some of the characteristics of a riddle-song; whisperingly, in a deep hush, we refer to each

aspect of creation, fruit, fish, bird, beast. We admit that man tries to dominate and destroy nature: which we contemplate with both wonder and fear.

If we are going to make music out of this poem we shall clearly have to start with the most rudimentary sound-material that Nature offers us. So we shall begin by listening to the silence that surrounds us. Two things, within the silence, we cannot help being aware of, and they are our recognition of the fact that we are, within the silence, alive. One is our awareness of our own breathing; the other is the tick of our beating pulse and the thud of our heart. Let us count out loud (but not very loud) the beat of our pulse. Let us exaggerate slightly the inhaling and exhaling of our breath, in time with the pulse, so that we can hear it. This is *our* sound, the breath of life; and for primitive peoples the sound of a creature, or even an object, is its soul, its essential substance.[3] We draw our breath from God, and must pay it back to him: for the fact of life—what indeed, in the modern phrase, makes us 'tick'—is the ultimate mystery.

Now when we have been breathing in and out like this for some time we shall find that we begin—without conscious intent—to give our breathings a kind of shape. Though we shall not turn breathing into song, it may easily become a sigh, a cry, a moan, bringing the vocal chords into play, involving two separate if indefinite pitches. Let us try this kind of breathing, and at the same time very softly tap or clap the rhythm of the pulse. Then let us play the pulse-beat on unpitched percussion instruments— if we have them: a large and a small gong, a suspended cymbal and a bass drum—keeping the sound so mysteriously soft, so quietly rustling and murmuring, that we can scarcely hear it, like this:

One might say that that is the noise that introduces

our beginning and rounds off our end. Nature has other resources to add to it. Sooner or later we shall discover a sound of definite pitch, for the boundary between the yell or moan and the sung tone is shadowy; or a metallic object, hit by chance with stick or stone, will ring like a bell. When this happens

and so sustain the tone for an indefinite period. Indeed the stops of an organ rich in mutations can be used to demonstrate overtone series in a more or less 'natural' state. In reproducing the tones of the Harmonic Series we have contacted the basic facts of the universe of sound:

we have discovered the basic acoustical laws of Nature; for in listening to a single, isolated pitched sound we unconsciously recognize that it is not in fact a single sound but a complex of sounds.[4] Sound consists of vibrations in the air, created by blowing through tubes (including the human larynx), or by hitting or scraping skin, wood, stone or metal; these vibrations excite complementary vibrations in the diaphragm of the ear; which in turn stimulate the nervous system. In what we call a single tone there is the fundamental note we blow or strike or scrape; there is also another tone vibrating twice to the fundamental's once; another vibrating three times to the fundamental's twice; another four times to the fundamental's three times; and so on, in an infinite sequence which we call the Harmonic Series. This is the natural law of sound, complementary to the visual law of the spectrum; and many of the lower members of the Harmonic Series (we call them overtones, or partials) are clearly audible when we strike, like this, a resonant bell or gong. We can hear them too if we sing or play (especially on an oboe, an instrument we describe as being rich in upper partials) a single note in a resonant building such as a church. But whether we consciously hear these tones or not, we cannot avoid being sub-consciously aware of them, so it is not surprising that (as we shall see) they condition the way in which music has grown up. For the moment, however, we are concerned merely with this acoustical law in itself, not with what man has done with it. We cannot very well sing the tones of the Harmonic Series because they would soon go beyond our compass; but we can play, and sustain, them on stringed instruments, if we have a large number of players; or if an organ were available we could, using very soft stops, hold down the notes with weights,

This is the sound that is eternally present, before our beginning and after our end. Whatever ancient peoples meant by the Music of the Spheres, this is certainly it.

Now let us repeat our heavy breathing and our slow pulse-beat on percussion and add, around and through it, this unchanging sound of the Harmonic Series, eternally present, infinitely soft (or as near to infinity as we can make it!). The sound of the Harmonic Series, the beat of the pulse, the inhaling and exhaling of breath: this is Nature's offering, from which we start. What does man, what can man, add to these resources? Rhythmically, he can add his own beat to, or even against, that of the pulse, generating excitement because the counterbeat seems to be a release from the domination of Time. Let us improvise some such rhythmic patterns and counter-patterns on such instruments as we have available, or simply by clapping or hitting (with a variety of sticks of different textures or with our palms or fists) bits of wood, metal or skin. It would be a good idea to write some of the patterns down, either in conventional notation or in a form of graphic or picture notation, as an aid to memory: for we shall have opportunities to introduce them into the piece we are creating. Many African peoples make music like this, and we are probably familiar with examples from jazz, which came in part from the African Negro. We might compare with our exercises some recorded examples, some of them from so-called primitive African drumming, which is often of great complexity; some from jazz drumming; and some from modern composers such as John Cage and Lou Harrison, who have been especially interested in reviving this largely forgotten musical resource.[5]

Such rhythmic composition may reach a point of

considerable sophistication. Rhythmic order may well be the first kind of order manifest in music: though we cannot say that music begins with rhythm since the most primitive types of music known to us are often rhythmically random, ignorant of periodic metre; and it seems that a sense of periodicity and recurrence grows alongside a development of man's vocal resources. Vocally, our first sounds will be cries that do not have intellectual meaning, though they are certainly expressive of feeling, whether of joy or pain. We have seen that these cries are usually indefinite in pitch; but certain patterns or formulae recur in the music of all primitive peoples, and it would seem that a descending yell moving approximately through the interval of a fourth is rooted deep in our physiology. After a while, however—and the while means many hundred or even several thousand years—we shall want also to give intelligible form to our consciousness, so that we can communicate with others. We shall invent the Word, a spoken language; and you will see from the text of the poem that the yells (yele, yao) are interspersed with meaningful words. So we shall form ourselves into two groups, one of which will deal with the brutish noises, while the other speaks the language. The latter is still at a rudimentary stage. Very tentatively, very softly, we shall whisper the words (over our pulse beat on percussion and our eternal sound of the Harmonic Series) in the groping rhythms of speech, like this:

The tree has giv-en its fruit and the fruit is good to

As yet we can hardly talk, let alone sing. We can use this as an exercise in choric speech; but when we come to a performance it will be more effective to have the words uttered by a solo speaker into a microphone. This will suggest our mysterious separation from the natural world, as though we are *growing towards* consciousness. It will have the further advantage of making the words audible.

The 'noises' chorus is, at this stage, more active. Obviously, the cries and yells are an extension of the heavy breathing we started from. We can get some ideas by listening to recordings of real primitive peoples, especially the American Indians;[6] though I do not suppose we shall need much prompting, for such cries are rooted in human and animal instinct. And gradually, being alive, being conscious, we grow more aware of the sounds of the animate world we live in. We discover that other manifestations of the natural world have their own kinds of speech too. Winds and waters seem to us to talk—to sigh and to babble; birds and beasts cry to express feeling and to communicate one with another; most insects and fish utter sounds which are audible and presumably meaningful to them, if not to us. Some very primitive peoples make a music not only out of their own sounds, but out of the sounds of the natural world: thunder, wind, water, above all the birds and beasts. In *being* the totem bird or beast they hunt or worship they become one with Nature and with the spirit of the ancestors: which they therefore need no longer fear. The bushmen of Australia and of Africa's Kalahari desert—perhaps the remotest and most primitive peoples still tenuously surviving—make a marvellously exciting medley of sounds in this way, which we might profitably listen to.[7] In a strict sense we could call such music heterophony, because it brings many voices together apparently at random, 'heterogeneously'; though the term heterophony is normally used to describe music in which several different versions of the *same tune* are performed simultaneously. The Beatles and other pop groups have used electronic tapes to produce bushman-type heterophony; we can make up some similar music ourselves. Using only our voices for the moment, let the younger among us be wailing winds and whirling waters, hooting owls, screeching parrots, barking foxes, snarling tigers, mewling cats, roaring lions, chattering monkeys, croaking frogs, and so on. Again, when we have produced some interesting combinations of sounds we might try to write them down in a graphic notation; we shall be able to use them in our composition.

For since we are not in fact primitives, but sophisticated modern people, even though some of us are young, we can elaborate more artistically the resources we have explored. Many of us will be able to play some musical instrument; which is one of the means man has invented to extend the resources of sound. All musical instruments are developments from the natural resources we have commented on: wind instruments (including organs) operate on the same principle as the human voice, stringed instruments by exciting vibrations in guts, xylophones by exciting vibrations in wood or metal; and so on. Instruments can be used most effectively to emulate the cries of birds and beasts. By removing the top joint of your recorder and rather gently blowing into it, making a descending slide, you can produce the most mysteriously hooting owls. By an upward slide on overblown horn you can make a barking fox or by slide on trombone a roaring rhinoceros. Flutes and clarinets in slow slides make mewling seagulls and/or cats; overblown flutes and clarinets can be squeaking mice, chittering rats and monkeys. You can add your own experiments to this menagerie; and also investigate the variety of wind and water noises you can make with variously struck and stroked cymbals and gongs. At a more developed stage you can invent (especially for woodwind and trumpets) short, reiterative phrases prompted by the cries of birds and beasts. The composer Messiaen offers a magnificent collection, and we should find it exciting and profitable to listen to some of them now.[8] I shall suggest a few 'cries' for various instruments—for flute, oboe, clarinet, bassoon, horn, trumpet, trombone and claves—which you can use as a basis for improvisation; and you can make up similar cries yourselves, writing them down, though not necessarily in normal notation.

We have now got all the material we need for this our first piece, so we shall begin to make it. We start with the beating pulse on soft percussion and the heavy breathing. We can keep this going for as long as our conductor thinks fit: until almost imperceptibly our piled-up tones of the Harmonic Series enter on muted strings, to be sustained indefinitely. Then the verbal cryings and yellings will begin in one chorus, the tentatively whispered words on the other (perhaps over a microphone). Very gradually we shall let the sounds of Nature—winds and waters, insects, birds and beasts—grow stronger and wilder, first on voices only, then on instruments too, using the phrases we have invented, repeated over and over, changed and modified if we wish. All the Nature-sounds proceed at random, in their own rhythm, without reference to one another or to the temporal pulse. We shall build up a tremendous hubbub, at odds with the pulse, not to mention the Harmonic Series! When the conductor thinks we can stand it no longer, he will break everything off, leaving only the sustained Harmonic Series (still very soft), the slow-beating pulse, and the voice whispering and crying in awe at the hurly-burly of the natural world. The division, the duality, of Man and Nature cannot, at this primitive stage, be resolved; and I suppose that what we have 'expressed' in this piece is man's fear of the unknown,

and his pathetic desire to control Nature's turbulence. He wants to make Nature serve him—as food, as beast of burden, and so on. In this piece it does not happen; which is why the piece has no 'form' and ends where it began, to be eternally repeated. As he grows up, however, man may begin in part to control nature. How he does so is remarkably similar in the history of the human race, and in the individual's growth from babyhood to age. This process we shall begin to trace in our next piece.

2

'Nature-Song' has consisted mostly of sounds, noises, of indefinite pitch and of pitches which, if they exist, remain motionless, going neither forward nor back. Even the pitch-sequences—cries, phrases rather than tunes—we invented for the birds and beasts were short, self-enclosed, continually repetitive, getting nowhere. But there is one thing that man can do that other animate creatures cannot: though some think birds can, to a point. This is to create a sequence of pitches in time that *goes on*. This would seem to be an aural representation of the life-process, growing like a flower or tree: so it is hardly surprising that many ancient peoples, both primitive and civilized, believed that in creating what we have come to call *melody* they were entering into a state of ecstacy. Indeed a melody almost becomes identified with the concept of the soul, and to make, or to discover in vision or dream, one's melody is to possess one's secret self, to become part of the cosmos, and therefore acceptable to God.

Assuming we are no longer content with the animal yell, yet are still in an aboriginal state, close to Nature, can we say anything about the kind of melody we should be likely to make?[9] At least there is a good deal of evidence that ancient peoples all over the world, and people in rural folk cultures down to the present day, seem to have used the same pitch sequences when they are creating melody unaccompanied and untrammelled; and the improvised singing of young children today, even in big industrial cities, supports this evidence. In order to understand the kind of melody we would make up if we lived in a state of 'nature' we must go back to our acoustical fact of the Harmonic Series. You will remember that when we sing a single tone, say middle C, we are also setting in motion other sound-vibrations in the ratios of 2 to 1, 3 to 2, 4 to 3 and so on; and that quite a number of these upper partials are audible to the naked ear (their number, indeed, conditions the quality of a sound, which is why middle C played on a flute sounds different from the same tone played on an oboe). This means that we cannot sing pitched sounds without being sub-consciously aware of the 2 to 1 relationship (the interval we call the octave: let us sing it); of the 3 to 2 relationships (the interval we call the fifth); and of the 4 to 3 relationship (the interval we call the fourth). If this is so, the enormous importance of these intervals in all primitive music (including that of young children), and in most purely melodic music, is easy to understand. Indeed, a great deal of ancient monodic music (the term monody simply means melody in a single line) consists of embellishments around these tones which, if we place them within the octave, are at this pitch C, F, G, c.

Another characteristic of these intervals is that the difference between the fourth and the fifth defines the interval of the tone: it is not arbitrary that in making melodies we tend to move up or down by that 'step' rather than another. The natural interval relationships themselves define the space we normally move through; and you can still sometimes hear (especially in Wales!) a preacher whose spoken declamation will fluctuate between two adjacent tones, introducing at points of climax a leap or fall of fifth or fourth. Such formulae are among the bases of any monodic music.

Now it would seem that in the beginnings melody evolved through an interaction of the two principles we have just described. The first principle is that of the acoustical importance of the fifth and fourth, and this kind of melodic gambit is a more coherently pitched version of the animal cry or yell. The phrases usually begin fairly high and descend through a fourth, fifth, or sometimes octave. The great musicologist Curt Sachs called them 'tumbling strains', and described them as 'pathogenic' because they stem direct from feelings, whether of joy, anger or fear. They tend therefore to be naturalistic, realistic, aggressive, male: associated with patriarchal societies. The second basic principle is that of the repeated tone and of an oscillation between two tones a step apart. Sachs called these 'undulating strains', which are 'logogenic' because they derive from the spoken word. They tend towards abstract pattern making rather than to naturalistic imitation; an aural counterpart to strings of beads or the reiterated patterns on primitive basket-work. They incline to be idealistic, decorative, passive, female: associated with matriarchal societies. Of course the male and female types of melody (which have their complements in 'open' linear male dances and in 'closed' circular female dances) are hardly ever found in their pure form. In the female type the words may sometimes excite the music into more aggressively male gestures; while the dynamic energy of the male type may be tamed and smoothed out into reiterated pattern. But it is from their interplay that melody germinates; and we shall find (unconscious) evidence of this in the tunes we shall be inventing during the course of this piece.

So far the melodic 'gambits' we have referred to contain no more than three, or possibly four, tones, which we can name C, F, G, c. But the more Man became *aware* of melody as in some sense a human creation, beyond the shout or yell, the more urgent is the need to extend the melodies, to achieve continuity. Some primitive peoples (especially the Africans) include in their opening 'gambits' higher members of the Harmonic Series, notably the major third; so that they employ, in addition to the original tumbling and undulating strains, fanfare-like phrases founded on the tones of the triad—C, E, G, c. This gives the music great energy and vivacity but does little to enhance the phrases' length and flexibility. More important is the unconscious process whereby man seems to have added new fifths and fourths to his original fifth and fourth, thereby arriving at more extended five note figures which we now call the pentatonic scale. In one of its several forms:

this scale is the basis of almost all primitive and civilized single-line musics. Of course a scale—as an ascending or descending sequence of tones—is only an abstraction, something *made out of* the phrases the voice naturally wants to sing. But there seems to be no doubt that such five-tone figures come most readily to the human voice: as is evident in the fact that some primitive peoples who are clearly familiar (from their instruments) with complete diatonic and even chromatic scales none the less *select* the pentatonic formulae for their tunes. (This is corroborated by experience with young children, who will make pentatonic tunes on xylophones and glockenspiels even though the entire chromatic range is available to them.) This being so, we shall not be surprised to find that pentatonic tunes, moving by full tone steps or by minor thirds, dominate musics as extreme and diverse as those of the Australian Bush, Africa, India, China, Japan, medieval Provence, Palestine, and English and American folk-cultures. Nor shall we be surprised to find that when the 'higher' cultures began to extend melody beyond the hypnotically repeated yell they used the pentatonic formulae in relatively free and unmeasured rhythm, annihilating the beat of Time. We shall listen to a few examples, beginning with the most primitive, moving on to oriental and Christian chant, and ending up with a song of the Beatles.[10] All these melodies are unaccompanied, or accompanied only by a drone, a continuously sustained tone which, in oriental cultures, symbolizes eternity. And all the songs are an act of worship, concerned with 'surrendering to the void' in order to induce ecstacy. In so far as they do this, carrying us 'out of ourselves', they help us to confront the terrors of the non-human natural world—that fear of the unknown which was the mainspring of our first piece.

So for our single-line melody we shall choose a poem where Nature is seen not as hostile to man, but as the origin of life, our perpetual renewal and support. It is a hymn to the sun, without which life on earth could not exist; and it is also about the dawn of a new day, the rebirth of light from night, which promises fresh warmth and hope within our hearts as well as in the outside world. This is the poem:

The day breaks—the first rays of the rising Sun,
    stretching her arms.
Daylight breaking, as the Sun rises to her feet,
Sun rising scattering the darkness, lighting up the land.
People are moving about, talking, feeling the warmth,
Burning through the gorge she rises, walking westwards,
Wearing her waistband of human hair.
She shines on the blossoming tree, with its sprawling
    roots,
Its shady branches spreading.

We want this song to be the quintessence of melody, so we shall have as many voices as possible chanting the tune in unison: we all become one in worshipping the godly sun. But we shall also have a 'noise' chorus of shouters, reinforcing words like 'shine' with ecstatic yells; and the middle section—which deals with people on the earth and is more difficult—we

shall give to a more expert semi-chorus of trebles and altos. It would sound fine to double the melody with brass instruments, which may sometimes stay still on bagpipe-like drone notes, while the voices move. We shall halo the melody with a shimmering of bells and percussion—gongs, cymbals, triangles—making a brilliant, sun-like crackling and sparkling this time, instead of a mysterious rustle.

In rhythm our melody must be very free, without bar-lines, because in hymning the sun we want to destroy the sense of time and mortality which is suggested by a recurrent beat. We shall let the line flow on in rhythms prompted by the way we should speak the words, yet repeatedly breaking into vocalize or melisma (many notes on a single syllable), because the spoken word is turning into air-borne lyrical song. We shall use the pentatonic formulae as a basis, but perhaps, not being in fact primitive peoples, we do not need to keep to them strictly. Anyway, we shall use them at two pitches a semitone apart; and as the sun rises we shall increase the excitement by bringing in bongo drums as support to the unpitched, unmeasured percussion. Of course, this means that the rhythm will begin to become more ordered, though we shall keep it flexible and flowing. The more measured rhythm reflects man's growing self-confidence: he is no longer dominated by Time's beat, but may impose his own rhythms upon it. By the end of our sun-hymn the rhythm will have become regular: though not in the duple rhythm of the pulse, but in a five-measure—which has a magic significance for many peoples. The growth towards a more regular rhythm throughout the song affects the nature of the form too. As we have seen, the point of monody such as this is that it should be a continuous, unbroken unfolding of melodic line. None the less, when the bongos appear we seem to have created something like a new 'section', with a different drone note (I suspect it may have been prompted by the fact that the words turn momentarily from the heavenly sun to people walking about on the earth); and when the music returns to the original drone notes and to the shining sun there is a free, modified repetition of the opening phrases. We can reinforce this sense of a consummation by an instrumental coda or tail-piece.

3

Formal elements become more important in the next

song, and this is not surprising, because it is about a human birth. You will see from the verses, which we shall read now, that this is not a mystical song, like the sun-hymn. It gives thanks to Nature, and maybe seeks to propitiate her; but mainly it is a celebration of human fertility and a hope for the child's future:

> A man child is born,
> A man child is born,
> May he live and be beautiful.
> A man child is born,
> A man child is born,
> May he become old, very old,
> Joy, joy, praise, praise!
> Ngongonabarota, know it, is his name!

We have already seen that so-called savage peoples often express joy and exuberance by counter-pointing several different rhythms against a steady pulse. This time we shall make a much more powerful and physical use of this technique, and we shall relate the counterpointing of rhythms to another primitive technique called antiphony: the cumulative building up of a structure through repetition, the brief phrases being tossed to and fro between a leader and chorus. We might listen to some examples of this from equatorial Africa.[11]

Our 'Birth-Song' is basically in a two-pulse, though sometimes it acquires an extra half-beat which gives the music a physical 'kick' which singers, as well as dancers, might well act in performance. It is started off by our large choral group (as many voices as possible), and the tune—far from being freely ecstatic like the 'Sun-Song'—is short, hard and fierce, with a narrow compass of only four tones (that rudimentary fourth again!), repeated over and over, as though we are trying to *force* the gods to fulfil our wishes for the child's future. We shall double the tune by instruments, preferably two trumpets, and let the voices divide in contrary motion. But they will always come back to their 'nodal' points of D and G, and the effect of any clashes they or the instrumental parts make will be percussive, reinforcing the drums. Against this singing chorus we shall place the second chorus which does not in fact sing, but shouts rhythmically supported by hard, sharp drumming and sometimes by cymbals and wind instruments.

So we have started off our paean to human birth in hypnotically reiterated melody, reinforced by percussive rhythm. When we come to the words about the child's future ('may he live and be beau-

tiful') it seems appropriate that the music should become more lyrical and flowing: so we shall let the line move in whole-tone steps over a much wider compass and we shall have this performed (both because it is longer, more intimate, and more difficult and because it needs more conventionally beautiful singing) by our more expert semi-chorus. The whole tones will remind us of the pentatonic formulae of the 'Sun-Song', but will sound more restless, less stable. There is a harmonic reason for this which we do not understand yet, though we shall do later. Because of this instability the flowing melody seems joyful, but also a bit frenzied, for we know how vulnerable the little man-child is, in the wastes of the world. The lyricism is abruptly destroyed by the full chorus's re-statement of the man-child refrain and the stamping rhythms, as we beat the earth with our feet. The semi-chorus responds with another 'hopeful' phrase ('may he become old, very old'), more extended in its lyricism, perhaps doubled by singing strings. Chorus and semi-chorus fuse in an outburst of joy and praise in regular rhythm, the voices dividing into two parts. At the end we return to the stamping and banging rhythm for the naming of the child—a deeply significant matter for primitive peoples, for the spoken intonation of the name is identical with the 'secret melody' that is the soul. We should note that whereas the primitive conception of form is simply incremental repetition which continues as long as the music is *useful* (for dancing to, for inducing frenzy, for propitiating the ancestors or what else). the form of this piece has become slightly more complicated. Taking over the idea of antiphony between leader and chorus, it creates an antiphony between the poem's festive celebration and its slightly fearful hope. The stamping refrain is the celebration, the stepwise flowing figure the hope; and the piece becomes a primitive kind of round or rondo—A, B, A1, B1, A2, B2, wherein A is the refrain and B the episode.

4

The 'Birth-Song' has been an outpouring of energy: the labour of being born, and man's assertiveness and combativeness in keeping going. The other pole of our natures is sleep wherein, emulating the quiet of death, we recharge our physical bodies by a descent into the subconscious world of dream. The

Pygmies' lovely little poem relates the nourishment of sleep to potential growth, like this:

> Sleep, sleep, little one, close your eyes, sleep little one!
> The night comes down, the hour has come, tomorrow
>   it will be day.
> Sleep, sleep, little one! On your closed eyes day has fled.
> You are warm. You have drunk, sleep, sleep, little one!
> Sleep, tomorrow you will be big, you will be strong.
> Sleep, tomorrow you will take the bow and knife.
> Sleep, you will be strong, you will be straight, and I bent.
> Sleep, tomorrow it is you, but it is mother always.

The verbal rhythms become hypnotic; and there are two musical means of inducing hypnosis, which have been used by primitive peoples down the ages. One is to repeat a rhythm gently but insistently, over and over; the other is to anchor the music to a drone or drones, which is the stillness of eternity. We shall give this tune, obviously, to our semi-chorus of girls, who become mother crooning to the new-born baby; and other voices may hum a descant if they wish. We shall make the rhythm triple, not duple: because whereas duple rhythms are the fundamental beat of the pulse, triple rhythms have for centuries been associated with the human act of breathing which, as we go about our lives, may seem to involve three stages: in, hold, out. Our drone-note, C, we shall sustain, preferably on cello, more or less throughout the song; we shall also use our other 'fundamental' notes of fourth and fifth (F and C) as drones, and we shall make a recurring pattern built around them, yet bringing in too a number of decorative notes. Above the G we shall add an A flat, which wants to fall to G like a sigh; above the C we shall add a D which may fall to the C or may rise through a minor third (pentatonically) to the F; and we shall also add a B natural which wants to 'lean up' to the C. So the notes are as follows:

and the pattern we make out of them is this:

which we could most effectively play on muted strings, the most humanly expressive of instruments. You should *feel* that A flat wanting to droop to the G, the B natural feeling upwards to C, but not getting there.

If we play this *ostinato*—the term simply means a pattern obstinately repeated—over and over its effect will be restful and trance-like. Yet the 'decorative' extra notes will have made it much more expressive, and intense, than if it had been built merely out of C, F and G (so 'decorative' is really an inadequate word to describe them). How appropriate this expressive quality is will be evident if we re-read the poem, which is neither an animal yell of energy like the 'Birth-Song' poem, nor an ecstatic paean, carrying us out of ourselves, like the 'Sun-Song': it is full of the mother's human tenderness for her baby; of hope for his maturity; and even of regret at the thought of herself grown older, and inevitably separated from her son. The *ostinato*'s hints of yearning (the upward leaning-tone), and of regret (the falling-tone) thus grow out of the human situations; and the tune that we make for the mother to sing should do so also. The more complex emotions of the poem couldn't be contained in a basic four-note reiteration like that of the 'Birth-Song', nor even in the flowing pentatonic melody of the 'Sun-Song'. So we shall make a tender, lyrical, female tune, moving mainly by step, but incorporating the semitonic falling notes of the *ostinato*. If we sing this descending scale:

we shall feel how the important, pivot notes are C, F, G, and c; and we shall feel the weight of the A flat and D flat sagging down to the G and C. Similarly, if we sing this scale:

we shall sense the upward lean of the D natural and F sharp; and the upward seeking B natural will seem the more melancholy for being in the falling version. Scales similar to this, intensifying pentatonic progressions with 'added tones', are common in oriental musics and in most folk musics, and probably the intensifying 'extra' notes ought to be sung rather sharper or flatter (according to whether they are looking up or down) than they would be in our equal tempered scales. We should sing them as though they hurt a little, giving the tune a pathos we have not touched on before, though without seriously disturbing its tranquillity. It sends us to sleep even as it reminds us of what it is like, or going to be like, to be human.

Formally this song is simply conditioned by the *ostinato*. But the first phrase of the melody might be thought of as a female version of the 'tumbling strain' such as is found in much primitive music. Starting on a high note, it descends to a point of repose: but does so by gentle step-movement rather than by leaps, and is rounded off by octave repetitions of the key-note. The second stanza begins a third higher but does not simply fall. Instead it 'undulates' through the ascending version of the scale pattern, as it imagines the child growing big and strong. Thought of the child entering the great unknown world momentarily stops the *ostinato*; when it starts again the tune inverts its original behaviour, beginning with a rise, with expressive leaning-notes, and then declining. The *ostinato* ceases when she says 'Tomorrow it is you', and the vocal line again breaks the swaying lullaby movement. The final broken phrase droops down to the keynote C, while the *ostinato* swings to stillness, yet remains unresolved. An instrumental coda transforms the rocking figure into pentatonic oscillations which introduce the carillon to the next piece.

5

The baby grows up, and in so doing discovers—as had been hinted in the lullaby—what living is about. Of course he falls in love and marries, renewing the circle by himself creating life. Sexual love is an ecstacy that also brings pain: the joy of being together, resolving twoness in oneness; the fear of loss and betrayal. The pygmies' beautiful poem would seem to call for the ecstacy we explored in the 'Sun-Song', and also for the pathos that was beneath the tranquil surface of the 'Sleep-Song':

My betrothed,
My beloved,
I leave you now.
Do not sorrow too much for me.
I cannot forget you.
Your eyes full of tears
Are the image of your heart.
All who love one another
Find it hard to part from one another,
And when we have held our marriage
We shall never part from one another again.

Obviously, in setting this, we must start with the ecstacy, creating a melody growing out of pentatonic

floatings and soarings, yet with considerable energy and power expressed through big leaps. Indeed, it should combine the characteristics of the male 'tumbling strain' with those of the female 'undulating strain'; and should be sung by a soloist with a broken voice (low tenor or high baritone), since the experience is becoming intimate and personal—one man addressing one girl—rather than communal.

Our 'pivot notes' will be F and C again; but we shall add the B flat below rather than the G above, making F rather than C the tonic to our pentatonic phrases:

We shall prelude the song with an instrumental introduction on pitched bells playing pentatonic twanglings on B flat, C, E flat and F, with celebrative arabesques on woodwind. When the voice enters, his line may be supported by oboes; and the winging melodies may soar over a drone on F and C, played by horns if we have them. Rhythmically the song should feel very free, like the 'Sun-Song', though we shall give it a basic five-pulse, a metre that is supposed to have magical properties. The vocal tune begins as a passionate salutation to the girl, followed by a drooping chromatic descent when he says he must leave her; the phrase for 'do not sorrow too much for me' should sound like a sigh and feel like plopping tears. The Gs, in the descending patterns, are often flattened into 'leaning-tones', giving the song a tension which the 'Sun-Song' did not have. Moreover, the G flats should probably be sung slightly flatter than they sound on an equal-tempered piano, scrunching down on to the Fs.

When the ceremonial address is repeated there is a difference, for the rising scale figure *stays* up; and after an instrumental interlude leads to the final stanza which says that the time will come when they need never part again. The voice part is different too. Since the words tell how love's certainty gets the better of pain, the melody has a sharpened upward leaning-note from B natural to C, instead of the falling-notes drooping from G flat to F. Pathos is still evident, because the B naturals make a sharp dissonance with the C of the drone. None the less there is a sense of upward resolution and release; which becomes stronger when the B naturals move not only up to C but also down to A natural. This creates with the drone notes a true harmonic resolution—the major third that is the next interval in the Harmonic Series, after the fifth and fourth. This makes the triad (F, A, C in this key) which we have not before experienced in these songs. We are entering a new world, in music as well as in human experience; but somewhat uneasily and warily, as the unresolved B natural which is the singer's last note suggests.

This song is basically a monodic chant which sometimes goes into two-part instrumental polyphony. This is appropriate enough for an experience that concerns two people.

6

We have said that the 'Love-Song', being a new experience, brings with it a new kind of musical technique—the phenomenon we call harmony, which is a fairly late and sophisticated development in musical consciousness and is, moreover, roughly restricted to Europe (and her American baby). Before we explore this more thoroughly in the next two songs, some further explanation is called for.[13] You will remember that we began, in the first song, with noise (which is chaotic or arbitrary sound) in silence; we proceeded to melody unaccompanied; and discovered that the basic melodic 'shapes' tend to be pentatonic, since these are the formulae derived mostly directly from the Harmonic Series. In adding 'falling tones' and 'leaning tones' to our basic series we have also discovered, however, that even within single line melodies some intervals produce a greater sense of tension or strain than others. We have noted that if we sing the note middle C and follow it by the c an octave above the effect will be stable and unperturbed, because the bottom tone vibrates once to the upper tone's twice, so that every alternative vibration coincides; the diaphragm of the ear—and the nerves attached to it—thus vibrates regularly. Similarly, if we follow our middle C with the G a fifth above, or the F a fourth above, the effect will remain stable and clear, for the vibration ratios (3 to 2 and 4 to 3) are still simple. But if we follow middle C with the b a seventh above, it will sound incomplete and unresolved. The effect will be one of tension and strain, for the upper tone now vibrates 15 times to the bottom tone's 8; the waves thus hardly ever coincide, and our nervous system is disturbed.

This is the crudest possible example of what is happening in music all the time: the relationships between different tones affect us as being 'concordant' or 'discordant', relaxed or tense, according to the vibration rates they bear to one another. The tones C to b referred to a moment ago are an interval, not a melody. But suppose we add another tone and proceed from C to b and then up to c, like this: Now we have a building up of tension, followed by a relaxation—the seventh resolved into the octave. Here we have a very simple example of melodic structure, and all melodies depend, in varying degrees of complexity, on the same principle. We have seen that, for acoustical reasons, pentatonic melodies have the minimum of tension; which is why they come spontaneously to children, to primitive peoples, and to sophisticated peoples in a state of bliss. We have also noted that as soon as melodies grow a little more complex through the introduction of so-called notes of 'embellishment' or decoration, they can hardly avoid introducing also some degree of tension. The falling-tones and leaning-tones in our 'Sleep-Song' and 'Love-Song' did not destroy the melodies' roots in octave, fifth and fourth; but they certainly changed, and intensified, our response.

St Augustine defined music as *ars bene movendi*—the art of moving well. By its very nature music involves movement in time, and it is obvious that in music written in a single unaccompanied line the effect of the interplay of tension and relaxation depends on the speed at which the intervals follow one another. The sustained leaning-tones in 'Sleep-Song' sound more poignant than the quicker ones in 'Love-Song' simply because they have longer to make their presence felt; or one could put it another way and say that in 'Love-Song' the singer is more concerned with the ecstacy he is feeling than with the underlying pain. Now if the relationship between tempo and tension is important in purely melodic music, still more is it important in harmonized music, in which two or more tones are sounded not successively but at the same time. All harmonized music—most of the music of Europe since the Renaissance—depends on an equilibrium between intervals of a high degree of tension (dissonances) and those of a low degree of tension (consonances), the degree being judged according to the vibration ratios of the tones that make up the chord. Moreover it is obvious that in harmonized music the 'form' of the whole will depend on the points in time at which the various plays of tension and relaxation take place. In 'Sleep-Song' the effect partly depends on the fact that in the last version of the lullaby tune there are more tones that bump dissonantly into the tones of the *ostinato* than there are on its first statement. Similarly, in 'Love-Song' the acuter, harsher leaning-tones of the second half prepare the way for the (almost) fulfilled resolution into a major triad at the end. It is easy to see that this effect depends essentially on the *time at which it happens*: because tension has been built up, we feel the need for its resolution.

Later in European music the whole theory of tonality evolved out of these physiological facts: tonality became the means whereby composers attempted to organize in time the aural relations between tension and relaxation. Our intervals of octave, fifth and fourth remained basic; but in harmonized music they became also related but contrasted 'centres' that came to be called tonic, dominant, and subdominant. The tonic is the centre of the fundamental tone we start from; the dominant dominates it by being a fifth higher; and the 'sub' dominant is a fifth beneath (which is the same as a fourth above). Tension is generated and controlled by departures from and returns to these centres; and the complex forms of classical European music—notably the sonata—are entirely dependent on them. In our 'creative experiments in sound'—which are concerned with the origins, the sources and resources of music—we shall not embark on these perilous seas. We should, however, recognize that the subsequent history of music is, as it were, latent in our discoveries; as will be evident in our next piece, 'Bride-Song', which deals directly with the process of growing up. Here is the poem:

> Slowly, slowly,
> Child, counting your steps,
> Go away, go away with tears,
> With a large heart, with a weary heart,
> Without turning your face,
> From the house, from the village,
> Where your eyes so gaily
> Laughed at every corner.
>
> Counting, counting your steps,
> Today you go away,
> With a large heart, with a weary heart,
> Go away, go away below.
> Counting, counting your steps,
> With a large heart, with a weary heart,
> Today you go away.

> Keep on your heart
> And guard well the flower
> Of your mother's garden,
> The flower which will say to you:
> 'I am still loved below'.
> Keep on your heart
> And guard well the flower
> In memory forever.
>
> Counting, counting your steps,
> Today you go away,
> With a large heart, with a weary heart,
> Go away, go away below.
> With a large heart, with a weary heart,
> Today you go away.

Clearly this melody must be given to the girls' semi-chorus: for it is sung by the mother, or maybe the parents, of the girl who is getting married, and describes her fear and distress at leaving the security of home. As so often in primitive cultures it presents a quite complex psychological state in physical terms, imitating the dragging, reluctant rhythm with which the girl walks away from safety, into the unknown. Of course the poem admits that that is what she has to do; but also advises her to keep alive the flower of her mother's garden, preserving innocence as she enters experience.

It is evident that she—or we—have not completely broken away from the *ostinato* pattern that ties us to home; none the less, the *ostinato* seems to have come out as tonally ambiguous as compared with our previous examples. It merges both the C, F, G pattern and also the B flat, E flat F pattern we have used in previous songs; by itself the *ostinato* looks more C-ish than B flat-ish, but the tonal root of the melody is probably B flat and, when the *ostinato* temporarily stops, the melody is definitely centred on B flat, but in a seven-note mode, like this:

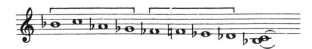

The fact that we employ a seven-note scale, rather than a three-, four- or five-note figure with 'added' tones, suggests that we are now thinking more harmonically; and this is reinforced by our (spontaneous) choice of a mode which has a flattened fifth. In the Middle Ages the fifth and fourth (which is the fifth inverted) were God's intervals, because they were, after the octave which is hardly a harmony at all, the most perfect consonances; the imperfect fifth or fourth (C to G flat, or C to F sharp) was the devil's interval, because it threatened tonal stability.

Our fifth-flattened melody, in its dragging rhythm, can hardly avoid—for all its stepwise movement—suggesting anguish and pain.

In addition to the tense intervals (imperfect fifths, major sevenths) within the melody itself, the vocal line creates recurrent clashes with the *ostinato*: the plangent, wailing sound and the thick texture of the accompaniment suggests a doubling of the voice by oboe, and dark bassoons, horns and low strings for the *ostinato*. The middle section of the poem, however, looking dreamily back to the innocence of childhood's garden, suggests a musical middle section which is a contrast to the lament; and this notion of opposing one state of mind against another is itself pretty sophisticated as compared with the techniques we have used previously. For the dreamy middle section we shall stop even any implied harmonic movement by playing the chords of tonic, dominant and subdominant—which are to become the main means of progression in European music—simultaneously, sustained on very soft strings. We shall centre the vocal melody around F, the upper fifth to B flat, so that it will seem brighter, lighter, more radiant than the lament; and we shall change the mode to one with clear major thirds, tender flat sevenths, and a considerable number of 'innocent' pentatonic figurations, since this is a reversion to a childish past. Pentatonic twiddles on bells are also appropriate; but they are banished when we return to the dragging, processional movement associated with 'counting the steps'. So we have come to accept the present, embracing within it memory of the past; and out of it have created a simple musical form of the type that came to be called ternary—for the obvious reason that it comprises three sections, A, B, A. Under the title of *aria da capo* this became one of the basic structures in European music before the sonata; and it is interesting to note how often, in eighteenth-century operas, the middle section of an *aria da capo* is concerned with memory of happiness lost, as compared with the present's harsh reality. Our *da capo* of the 'lament' is shortened, but fairly strict. I feel, however, that it ought to fade away into nothingness: because after all this end (the girl is leaving home) is also a beginning (her entry into her new life).

7

So far, our experience of growing up has been painful: in the lament we are more aware of what we have lost in passing out of childhood than of what we have gained. The next piece, 'Living-Song', concerned with the contradictory emotions in being grown-up in an adult world, is, if equivocal, more positive. Let us read it:

> It is lovely to put together
> A bit of a song,
> Avaya,
> But I often do it badly, avaya!
> It is lovely to hunt,
> But I seldom shine like a burning wick
> On the ice, avaya.
> It is lovely to have wishes fulfilled,
> But they all slip past me!
> It is all so difficult, avayaya!

For the most part the effect made by this poem is merry. It tells us that it is good to be alive, more or less in possession of our destiny ('It is lovely to put together a bit of a song'). But while it is fine to be able to create, we are also subject to human frailty ('I often do it badly'); and we have to admit that while it is 'lovely to have wishes fulfilled', we should be stupid to expect this to happen often. The delightful poem ends with the very modern-sounding words 'It is all so difficult'; and it is clear that to express in music such relatively complex emotions we shall have to call on all the resources we have so far explored; and probably to add to them.

The poem calls for an *ostinato* rhythm, for it is about going on, and the eskimos preserve many primitive qualities. It wants to be a lively rhythm, because we are happy to be alive, able to sing and create; but it should also be slightly nervous and jittery, because we are aware of the difficulties of being human. So let us start off with a quick *ostinato* in quintuple rhythm, on hard dry percussion, like this:

The tune ought to be gay and rhythmic, sung by semi-chorus, because it is quite tricky. We shall let it bounce out of the *ostinato* figure, centering it around the basic D and G which had characterized our 'Birth-Song', but allowing it to become more lyrical and expressive. The full chorus can join in with abandoned pentatonic yells on the exclamation Avaya!

But since the emotion is so much more complicated and sophisticated than the 'Birth-Song' we can expect more things to happen in the instrumental parts. The *ostinato* pattern on woodwind and *pizzicato* strings can begin with an oscillation between G and F and then, falling to E flat and C, can acquire dissonant figurations in contrary motion just before the 'Avayas'. The sound is perky, yet somewhat harsh and gritty too; and there is a further and more radical change at the bit about the difficulty, if not impossibility, of wishes being fulfilled. Perhaps we should think of this as an older, sadder and wiser version of the 'hopeful' episodes in the 'Birth-Song': whereas they had merely complicated the harmonic sense by introducing whole-tone movement that produced imperfect fifths, our wishfulness here makes us lose the anchor of our *ostinato* completely. The bass moves down A, G, F, E flat, D flat, C and then abruptly to A flat, which unexpectedly becomes our tonal centre for the passage about wishes fulfilled. We have, in fact, modulated from one key to another (at the fairly remote pitch of the flat major third). If you listen carefully you will see what a dreamy effect this has, especially since the melodies, both in the voice and in the instruments, here grow more lyrical and extended, more flowing, less jaunty. This particular modulation (to the major third below) is one that Schubert was fond of, and he associated it with a similar wistful relaxation. This is our first use of contrasted tonalities; which extends the alternations of tension and relaxation we have observed *within melodies* to all the elements that make up a musical whole.

Part of the effect here depends on a tension between the vocal nature of the melodies (with flat thirds and sevenths) and the sharp sevenths and thirds of the instrumental parts. It will probably sound rather blues-like and jazzy to you, and for good reason, since what happened in jazz was that the ancient, vocal behaviour of folk melody imported from Africa came into rewarding conflict with harmonic conventions derived from the music of modern Europe. The jazziness is preserved, perhaps enhanced, as we make a climax by expanding the *ostinato* figure from five to eight semiquavers a bar and then contracting it to seven, to six, to five. We are now back at the original figure; but the key-centre seems to have slipped to C rather than D. We counteract this falling tendency by increasingly vigorous yells of 'Avaya', in two parts, not one, creating some scrunchy harmonies. The chord accompanying the last vocal shout combines triads on C, D and G, making tonic, dominant and subdominant a simultaneous moment. The instrumental coda seems to have turned into a triple-rhythmed blues: which may indicate how 'modern' the eskimos' poem is.

<h1 style="text-align:center">8</h1>

Formally, 'Living-Song' consists of a series of verses with refrain: which modulate and *develop*, if not very far. So the technique, like the experience, is the most sophisticated we have yet explored. In combining a forward thrusting energy with frustration, however ironically expressed, it would seem to sum up the human lot; and in the next piece, 'Ageing-Song', the negative begins to triumph over the positive impulse. The charming poem, which we shall now read, tells how, growing old, we cannot get out into the great open air, or if we do, we 'faint away'; in hunting, we mean well, but 'usually make a hole in the ice at the wrong place':

I, who no longer move about indoors
And no longer get out
To the great open air, since last winter,
As I do nothing but faint away,
I who no longer move about outside—
Pastime in the open air usually gives meat,
Usually it is right!
I who no more get very far
On the great ice since last winter,
Because I do nothing but faint away,
My implement for hunting I have not used,
My fish-hook, since last winter.
And yet my stomach desires,
It longs for meat—poor me,
Who usually make a hole in the ice at the wrong place!

We have noted that up to this point our songs have been growing gradually more lyrical, more ordered in rhythm, more complex in harmony. This song of old age clearly ought to be the most complicated, the most 'experienced', in harmony and texture; while at the same time the rhythm begins to disintegrate, losing control, and the lyricism returns, at the end, to muttered speech. This song must essentially be sung by a soloist, with broken voice (low tenor or high baritone), for the point lies in the old man's separation from the communal group.

We shall begin with a drone-chord that consists of a perfect fourth and an imperfect fifth telescoped, like this:

Wagner's famous Tristan chord is the same, differently spaced; and the fusion of chords traditionally associated with God and the devil seems a fitting background to a piece about man's return to his origins! We can make a melodic complement to this by using a scale based on D, but involving both the perfect and the imperfect fifth—D to A and D to A flat, like this:

We shall use a basic seven pulse, rather long and attenuated, and keep the rhythm of the melody free and wavery, like seaweed floating on the tide, because we are losing command over our fate. Against the voice part we shall counterpoint two instrumental parts, mostly moving in parallel thirds, a more harmonically sophisticated interval than fourths or fifths, as we shall remember from our discussion of the Harmonic Series. We shall let the instrumental parts float in and out of the vocal line, threatening to wash it away completely. Yet because this is a song about experience, it very much exists in Time; and in form is a series of verses in each of which the ageing man rebels more against physical disintegration, which will not let him live his life as he once did. Each outburst grows more extended and elaborate in line and makes harder dissonances with the drone-chord: until at his ultimate expression of impotent rage, the drone-chord changes, making a true harmonic climax, and in so doing creating the most complex and difficult music we have yet invented. This outburst, however, seems finally to exhaust him. The instrumental parts slacken and subside in imperfect fifths, and the voice droops through whole tones on the words 'poor me', then disintegrating into speech. The rhythm is broken; the impulse lyrically to sing is defeated; and human life returns to its source.

A postlude to this song transforms the rhythmic irregularities into a weary waltz. The semi-chorus enters, keening a wordless elegy on age and dissolution; as we limply lose control the waltz rhythm slackens, and the melody changes into that of the lullaby that had been sung to the new-born babe, suggesting that our end is as our beginning. The melody also merges into the song of parting and journeying which had been the bride's lament: we are losing consciousness, entering on the longest journey and the big sleep that is death.

9

Death, indeed, is the theme of the final song, the poem of which is closely related to that of the 'Nature-Song' which had been our beginning:

> The animal runs, it passes, it dies.   And it is the great cold.
> It is the great cold of the night, it is the dark.
> The bird flies, it passes, it dies.   And it is the great cold.
> It is the great cold of the night, it is the dark.
> The fish flees, it passes, it dies.   And it is the great cold.
> It is the great cold of the night, it is the dark.
> Man eats, and sleeps.   He dies.   And it is the great cold.
> It is the great cold of the night, it is the dark.
> There is light in the sky, the eyes are extinguished, the star shines.
> The cold is below, the light is on high.
> The man has passed, the shade has vanished, the prisoner is free. Khvum, Khvum, come in answer to our call!

The 'Nature-Song' had celebrated, in mystery and awe, the natural world of plants, fish, birds and beasts and had wonderingly speculated about man's place in it. The 'Death-Song' starts from the end of each aspect of animate nature; but wrests comfort from the fact that Man's death seems to be part of an eternal cycle, perpetually renewed.

So we shall return to the 'Nature-Song's' undulating pulse, on very soft percussion. We shall make the pulse no less regular than in the first song, but somewhat slower, since it is running down. We shall accompany the pulse with note-clusters on strings and voices, these being half-way between notated pitches and noise; here we must sing and play quarter-tones as well as half-tones. The note-clusters combine pitches adjacent to both C and D. The speaker, using a microphone, begins by declaiming the words of the poem ('The animal runs, it passes, it dies') more or less in the manner of the first song; chorus and semi-chorus alternate (and overlap) in singing the refrains about the great cold of the night and the dark. These refrains are centred on D, but make semitonic clashes with long-held pedal notes, mostly on woodwind. The speaker raises declamation to a kind of runic incantation, paralleling the contours of the solo woodwind phrases that reflect the bird's flight and death. The same thing happens when the fish passes and dies, this time a fifth lower, on G rather than D. The choral refrains about the great cold remain, however, at the same pitch, and during all these verses about the decay of the natural world there is virtually no harmonic movement.

Only when we turn to man and recognize that he too eats and sleeps, passes and dies, entering the great cold, do we experience a momentary shock which quivers the music from D to C sharp. But when we see 'a light in the sky' the drone is broken for the first time, and there is the first real modulation, to G flat, which leads to a substitution of a pedal C (the 'root' of the first movement, 'Nature-Song') instead of D. The two choruses, divided, tell us that the cold is below and the light above; and we invoke the god Khvum to descend from the heavens and give us peace. This invocation is the first and only passage fully harmonized, in four parts, in the whole work. It is as though our humanity—our manhood—is fulfilled only in accepting our place in the scheme of things; and the movement, by whole tones, gradually subsides until it rests—

we should *feel* how this is lower, deeper, calmer, than the initial D—on a C major triad with added seconds and sevenths. This is part of the Harmonic Series (at the same pitch) which had been one of the origins of 'Nature-Song'. Imperceptibly, this chord of Nature takes over again until there is nothing except it and the slowly undulating pulse on percussion. The muttering and heavy breathing also return and then the nature-noises—winds, waters, birds and beasts—of the first movement, but now heard distantly, played backwards on electronic tape, since we are now dead. There is one other difference from 'Nature-Song': the noises are now dominated by a unison pitched middle C—the ultimate unity which is God. Beginning soft, this rises to maximum loudness and intensity on all instruments. Then it breaks off, leaving echoing gongs and reverberating silence through which the muttering and heavy breathing gradually subside. There is no longer any pulse. The final expiring breath—the Voice of God—should fade into a silence one can *feel*, before admitting that the work is over.

NOTES FOR TEACHERS

1 See Richard Slade, *Masks and How to Make Them* (Faber and Faber, 1964).

2 I found all the poems in C. M. Bowra's book *Primitive Song* (Weidenfeld and Nicholson, 1961). The translations are his, and I am grateful for his cooperation. His book provides a fascinating introduction to the anthropological and mythical implications of the texts, and of others related to them. Geography, history, English literature and drama classes will find here copious material relevant to this project, and exciting in itself: How do the values of these primitive peoples compare with ours? How do their notions of song differ from our more consciously aesthetic traditions? Bowra's book contains little or nothing about the music and dance which are inseparable from the words, but his book may be read in conjunction with others mentioned below, and in particular with Marius Schneider's chapter on primitive music in the *New Oxford History of Music*, and with Curt Sach's great book *A World History of the Dance* (Allen and Unwin, 1957; now available in paperback).

3 See chapter 1 of the *New Oxford History of Music;* and some of the bushmen myths recounted in Laurens van der Post's *The Heart of the Hunter* (Hogarth Press, 1961).

4 What follows is a grossly oversimplified account of the phenomenon of the Harmonic Series. It contains all that is immediately relevant to my composition; but I assume that the rudimentary laws of acoustics will already have been studied in the Physics class. Standard text-books are Sir James Jeans's *Science and Music* (Cambridge University Press, 1937; also available in paperback), Alexander Wood, *The Physics of Music* (Methuen University Paperbacks, 1962), C. A. Taylor, *Physics of Musical Sound* (English Universities Press, 1965), W. Bragg, *The World of Sound* (Bell, 1932). I hope that at this point Physics students will indulge in practical Pythagorean experiment and demonstration. This can also be related to the construction of musical instruments, some of which may be used in this piece.

5 The key record for African drumming is in the Ethnic Folkways series: *Drums of the Yoruba of Nigeria* EF 4441. The series also contains recordings of Maori and Haitian drumming. These records are, however, expensive, and not always easily obtainable. A few examples may be found in the four-volume Ethnic Folkways set called *Music of the World's Peoples*, which some schools possess. Almost any vintage Max Roach will serve as example of jazz drumming. The Cage and Harrison pieces are on a disc called *Concert Percussion* (TIME 58000): American, but obtainable.

6 Relevant records: *Music of Sioux and Navaho* FE 4401; *Indian Music of the Southwest* FW 8850.

7 *Music of the World's Peoples* contains a marvellous aboriginal Australian snake-song. Tribal music of Australia is on FE 4439 and the African Bushmen on FE 4503.

8 There's a readily available recording of Messiaen's *Chronochromie* which contains the famous 'dawn-chorus'. Several of the bird pieces are also recorded.

9 What follows is again a grossly oversimplified account of a very difficult subject. The sections on the origins of melody in chapter 1 of the *New Oxford History* are excellent; reference should also be made to chapter 1 of Bela Szabolcsi's *The History of Melody*, trans. Cynthia Jolly (Barrie and Rockliff, 1965), and to the relevant sections of Curt Sachs' *The Wellsprings of Music* (Martinus Nijhoff, the Hague, 1961) or *The Rise of Music in the Ancient World* (W. W. Norton, New York, 1943), and to Bruno Nettl's *Music in Primitive Culture* (Harvard University Press, 1956).

10 It is hardly necessary to specify recordings here. *Music of the World's Peoples* provides many examples which can be collated with available records of plainsong, troubadour song, Jewish cantillation, folk song and so on. The Beatle record I had in mind was 'Tomorrow never knows', on *Revolver* or the George Harrison number from *Sgt. Pepper;* but there are now innumerable examples in pop music, not to mention Modern Jazz, such as the later Coltrane.

11 There are examples in *African Music South of the Sahara* FE 4503.

12 Some cooperation might be possible between artists and scientists in investigating the biological and neurological effect of repeated patterns, audible, visual and tactile. Anyway, the musicians should experiment with sleep-inducing or trance-invoking ostinato patterns. Listen to John Cage's *She is Asleep* in his recorded retrospective concert. Incidentally the vocal part in this piece offers fascinating examples of a modern composer's use of primitive techniques of vocal production. Morton Feldman's *Piece for 4 Pianos* (and other works recorded on a TIME disc) may also be listened to. They induce hypnosis by relinquishing beat, rather than by reiterating it, the sounds being isolated in surrounding silence.

13 The comments that follow on tonality, harmony and modulation may seem ironically brief. It seems reasonable to assume, however, that a working knowledge of European harmonic tradition will have been the basis of most of the children's musical education. Here I have included only so much as was relevant to this more basic undertaking. The section may be expanded at will, and related to normal classroom work and whatever text books are in use. The chapters on sonata in A. Harman and W. Mellers *Man and his Music* (Barrie and Rockliff, 1957-60) could be helpfully referred to.

www.ingramcontent.com/pod-product-compliance
Ingram Content Group UK Ltd.
Pitfield, Milton Keynes, MK11 3LW, UK
UKHW052101280225
455719UK00014B/454